LEADERSHIP
SECRETS TO SUCCESS

MEN ON THE
EDGE

GARY HOFFMAN

Leadership Secrets to Success
Copyright © 2006, revised 2011 by Gary Hoffman

Requests for information should be addressed to:
Men On The Edge
PO Box 283
Trabuco Canyon, CA 92678
www.MenOnTheEdge.com

Available at:
      www.Amazon.com
      www.CreateSpace.com
      www.MenOnTheEdge.com

Library of Congress Cataloging-in-Publication Data

Leadership Secrets to Success / Gary Hoffman.
      p. cm. – Study Guide
      Includes bibliographical references.
      ISBN 0-9845421-2-4 (pbk.)

LCCN #2010913781

This publication is designed to provide accurate and authoritative information regarding the subject matter covered. It is sold with the understanding that the author or publisher are not engaged in rendering legal, accounting, or other professional services. If legal advice or other expert assistance is required, the services of a competent professional person should be sought.

Dear reader,

As you consider stepping into leadership of a men's or women's group, or if you are already serving in that capacity, this book offers some suggestions to help you improve your small group leadership and/or ministry leadership skills. The suggestions presented in this book are not foolproof, but they have helped our small groups, support groups, and ministry teams for several years. Know that with humility, as a servant leader for God, he can use *you* in an incredible way for eternity. We are all just ordinary people asked to do extraordinary things for his purposes. If we are willing, God takes us, expands us, and uses us as purified vessels for his Glory.

> *Praise be to the God and Father of our Lord Jesus Christ, the Father of compassion and the God of all comfort, who comforts us in all our troubles, so that we can comfort those in any trouble with the comfort we ourselves have received from God.* 2 Corinthians 1:3–4

In his service,

Gary Hoffman

LEADERSHIP

is not a magnetic personality

that can just as well be a glib tongue.

It is not "making friends and

influencing people"—that is flattery.

Leadership is

lifting a person's vision to higher sights,

raising a person's performance

to a higher standard and building

a personality beyond its normal limitations.

—Peter Drucker

CONTENTS

INTRODUCTION

The purpose of this leader's guide is to help develop effective leaders, for the Glory of God. Men and women who lead others provide spiritual support and growth opportunities for them, so that all may know God for eternity. This book is a tool for use by leadership teams and in small groups and support groups. As you learn and grow as a servant leader for God, he will help you care for the people he wants you to shepherd. He will teach you to:

Know Your Sheep,

Grow Your Sheep,

Show Your Sheep!

This guide will help you learn valuable secrets of successful small group leadership. In this leader's guide you will find tools to build or improve your skills as a leader, whether you lead a small group or a leadership team. You do not have to know all the answers, or be the smartest person in a room, to effectively lead others. A more important key to leading others is to *serve*—to make yourself available to be used by God for his Glory. With proper training, timing, and a humble, positive attitude, God will use an eager *available* servant every time. Learn to *surrender* to his plan. We all have abilities, talents, and gifts hidden deep inside us, just waiting to be uncovered. The *secret* is to trust in God to develop you, as you learn key ingredients to mentoring others in today's society; a greatly needed commodity for both men and women.

In our fast-paced stressful lives, people are hungry for honest and safe relationships in a group environment. In reading this book, you will learn some hidden treasures of group leadership, and you can play an important part in helping others grow and lead healthy, hopeful, God-centered lives. So step forward and let yourself be used by God to lead a small group or ministry team, mentoring those you touch along the way. Part I of this book provides keys to developing healthy ministry leaders. Part II of this book provides keys to developing and leading a healthy, growing small group.

Pray as you read the leadership secrets to success in this book, gaining God's wisdom and discernment to lead your group or leadership team. You will gain confidence and security day-by-day, with God guiding your group. A suggestion is to read and re-read this material. Ask God to show you what he wants you to learn. As revealed in James 1:5, all you have to do is pray and ask for his wisdom: *If any of you lacks wisdom, he should ask God, who gives generously to all without finding fault, and it will be given to him.*

I. LEADERSHIP CHARACTERISTICS OF A HEALTHY MINISTRY TEAM

Part of being a good men's or women's group leader is being part of a leadership team. An important part of your growth as a leader will happen as you become part of a ministry leadership team. As a team, God will use you to encourage each other and to help each other grow. As you interact and seek God's will for ministry, you will learn your responsibilities as a leader, leadership skills, teaching skills, and about teamwork.

As iron sharpens iron, so one man sharpens another. Proverbs 27:17

Functions and Responsibilities

1.   **Team mentoring in the group** – Encourage, with God's help, your group members to have their "Monday, Tuesday, Wednesday, Thursday, and Friday" group members around them, those of the group which rally around a group member in a time of crisis or need. These are other group members that they interact with on a frequent and regular basis. They are members of the group which rally around a hurting member, or a member who needs encouragement. They should carefully choose to spend time with Godly members that they admire and respect. They ought to encourage, mentor, lift up, and show accountability to each other.

Jesus replied: "Love the Lord your God with all your heart and with all your soul and with all your mind." This is the first and greatest commandment. And the second is like it: 'Love your neighbor as yourself.' All the Law and the Prophets hang on these two commandments." Matthew 22:37–40

7

2.   **Set a tone for growing and learning** – Encourage ways that group members and leaders can learn and grow. Good leaders are teachers. God knows your strengths and weaknesses. Good teachers teach by example. Do you have a book on your nightstand to feed your mind? Are you taking time to learn by going to marriage or relationship seminars or classes and joining Bible studies? These types of activities will help you on your journey to Godly wisdom and discernment. Also in our modern age of the internet, we have many other valuable ways of learning Godly information at a moment's notice, with e-books, daily devotionals, or daily studies that can come to you on your computer or phone.

And this is my prayer: that your love may abound more and more in knowledge and depth and blameless until the day of Christ, filled with the fruit of righteousness that comes through Jesus Christ—to the glory and praise of God. Philippians 1:9–11

3.   **Your ministry does not have to be mine** – God has given each of us a ministry, or possibly several key purposes in our life. It makes sense that my ministry is probably not yours; that your purpose may not be mine. Encourage the members in your group to find their purpose and their God-given ministry and make use of it during the time that they have here on Earth.

> Encourage the members in your group to find their purpose and their God-given ministry.

In a large house there are articles not only of gold and silver, but also of wood and clay; some are for noble purposes and some for ignoble. If a man cleanses himself from the latter, he will be an instrument for noble purposes, made holy, useful to the master and prepared to do any good work. 2 Timothy 2:20

4.   **Uncover your God-given gifts and talents** – We are all gifted in many areas, often more than we are aware of. In prayer, challenge God to show you, or put on your heart, what some of your gifts and hidden talents are. Stretch your comfort zone by facing your fears so that God can expand your gifts and talents. As time passes and as you use some of your hidden talents (which may seem foreign to you in the beginning) you will become more comfortable with your God-given gifts. An example might be that maybe you feel that you

are not a speaker, yet you find yourself sharing on a weekly basis to your small group. Maybe you find yourself writing studies or key thoughts to share with others. Learn to tap into the many, many valuable gifts and talents that God has set aside for you!

> *Each of you should use whatever gift he has received to serve others, faithfully administering God's grace in its various forms. If anyone speaks, he should do it as one speaking the very words of God. If anyone serves, he should do it with the strength God provides, so that in all things God may be praised through Jesus Christ. To him be the glory and the power for ever and ever. Amen.* 1 Peter 4:10–11

5. **Find others in ministry to accent your weaknesses** – It is impossible to know and be everything, so it is important to delegate and share areas of responsibility that are not your strong areas. Let your group members help you, and make your job easier. Pray for God to place a Godly group of members around you to assist the hurting in your group.

> *Do not fear, for I am with you; do not be dismayed, for I am your God. I will strengthen you and help you; I will uphold you with my righteous right hand.* Isaiah 41:109

What can you do today to make a difference for tomorrow?

6. **Growth is the key** – Is the group growing? Are you growing? Why not? You may ask, "Why is this person stuck or hung up?" As a group facilitator, challenge others to grow. Learn to encourage a group's growth and often the group will step into what you expect of them. If someone is stuck, you may have to try a different approach. Challenge the person by saying "What can you do today to make a difference for tomorrow?" Have them write it down. Follow up with them, and see the fruit of your encouragement to them.

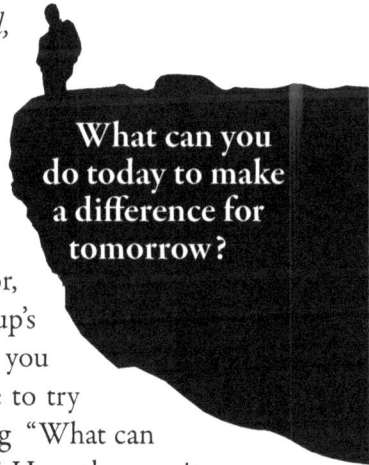

> *Serve wholeheartedly, as if you were serving the Lord, not men, because you know that the Lord will reward everyone for whatever good he does...* Ephesians 6:7–8

Leadership Skills

7. **Transparency of the leadership team in group meetings** – It is extremely important for the leaders of your small group to be real, honest, and transparent. If your group members cannot relate to you, you will be less effective as a leader. In a small group you will learn that you only need to be one step ahead of the group, delegating and learning as you grow. A good support group leader or small group leader usually has walked the narrow road, and by example shows others how to live a Godly life, modeling it in their own life. Learn to not take the role of leadership lightly, as there is a higher responsibility. God has higher standards for those who are in leadership as shown in these verses:

> *Anyone who breaks one of the least of these commandments and teaches others to do the same will be called least in the kingdom of heaven, but whoever practices and teaches these commands will be called great in the kingdom of heaven.* Matthew 5:19

> *Jesus said to his disciples: "Things that cause people to sin are bound to come, but woe to that person through whom they come.*
> *It would be better for him to be thrown into the sea with a millstone tied around his neck than for him to cause one of these little ones to sin.*
> *So watch yourselves."* Luke 17:1–3

8. **Humble leadership** – It is extremely important to have a humble, God-like attitude. Use Jesus Christ as your example as the Master Teacher. Jesus had a humble, servant-like attitude. Study Jesus Christ's teaching style as your ministry grows. A suggested small but powerful book to read is *Master Plan of Evangelism* by Robert E. Coleman.

> *Be shepherds of God's flock that is under your care, serving as overseers—not because you must, but because you are willing, as God wants you to be; not greedy for money, but eager to serve; not lording it over those entrusted to you, but being examples to the flock.*
> *And when the Chief shepherd appears, you will receive the crown of glory that will never fade away.* 1 Peter 5:2–4

9. Have high moral expectations for yourself and group members – Group members will absorb what they see; similar to a dry sponge becoming filled with water. Help them fill up with living water. It is extremely important that group members have leaders whose lives are as pure and clean as possible, since a lot of eyes are watching a leader's actions. You will observe new members quoting you and doing what you do. Raise your level of integrity and the moral bar for yourself, thus modeling a Godly example for your fellow leaders and your group.

Be careful that you do not forget the Lord your God, failing to observe his commands, his laws, and his decrees that I am giving you this day.
Deuteronomy 8:11

10. Face your fears in ministry – It is important to face your fears, those big giants in your ministry. Maybe it is public speaking, or writing, or sharing who you really are. As you pray, humbly lay your fears and shortcomings at the foot of the cross, so God can make you stronger when you face these giants. Soon you will see that these giants are not as big as they once appeared in your mind. Often you become more comfortable with your fears when you've faced them head on trusting God. As you step out in faith, he will use you to achieve his goals.

God is love. Whoever lives in love lives in God, and God in him.
In this way, love is made complete among us so that we will have
confidence on the day of judgment, because in this world
we are like him. There is no fear in love. But perfect love drives out
fear, because fear has to do with punishment. The one who fears is not
made perfect in love. 1 John 4:16–18

Often you become more comfortable with your fears when you've faced them head on trusting God.

11. Know that with God in your ministry, your ministry will not sink – How big is your God? Ultimately it is his ministry. Give him your group problems and shortcomings. God is a very creative God. He is able to expand our resources at a moment's notice. Your job is to be faithful and obedient and not to miss any opportunities that he sends your way.

Now faith is being sure of what we hope for and certain of what we do not see. This is what the ancients were commended for. By faith we understand that the universe was formed at God's command, so that what is seen was not made out of what is visible. Hebrews 1:1–3

12. Strive to be "God with skin on" in ministry – Make every attempt to have a Christ-like attitude in ministry. Learn to be a vessel, with the power of the Holy Spirit using you and guiding you. Try to have pure motives and as clean a life as possible, being as humble as possible in your responses and actions. God will use all of your past experiences to provide an incredible testimony for his glory. Your goal is to be "God with skin on" doing your best as humanly possible, having a Christ-like attitude in ministry and other areas of life.

> **Your goal is to be "God with skin on."**

Be imitators of God, therefore as dearly loved children and live a life of love, just as Christ loved us and gave himself up for us as a fragrant offering and sacrifice to God. Ephesians 5:1

13.   Be respectful of church doctrine and guidelines – If your ministry is tied to a specific church, it is extremely important to listen, follow, and to be respectful of your church, or church pastor's or church leader's requests. You may have a situation where you will not fully agree with what is being asked of you. Remember that pastors, church staff members, and church elders may know something that you don't know. Often they have past experience or a history in the area in question, or a tight budget accountable to the board or others. In time, as you wait on God, all things will eventually be brought into the light.

Keep the way of the Lord by doing what is right and just.
Genesis 18:19

The Lord abhors dishonest scales, but accurate weights are his delight.
Proverbs 11:1

14. Have pure motives in your ministry – Pray for and strive for pure motives and a pure agenda with God at the helm of your small group or support group. You might be surprised, as others will begin to model how you act. Stay away from hidden agendas of any kind so you can be used by God. As you do this, your ministry will grow and not be hindered by impure motives.

Strive for pure motives and a pure agenda with God at the helm.

Whoever can be trusted with very little can also be trusted with much, and whoever is dishonest with very little will also be dishonest with much. Luke 16:10

15. Do your utmost to be a healthy balanced person – It is important to balance family, work, ministry, and individual time with your spouse and children. If you are one-sided in any area of life, your small group can suffer. Pray and ask God to help you balance priorities in your life, your family, and your group, as God uses you for his purpose.

Be imitators of God, therefore, as dearly loved children and live a life of love, just as Christ loved us and gave himself up for us as a fragrant offering and sacrifice to God. Ephesians 5:1–2

Be careful, then how you live—not as unwise, making the most of every opportunity, because the days are evil. Therefore do not be foolish, but understand what the Lord's will is. Ephesians 5:15–17

16. Know your limitations physically and emotionally – A small group ministry can be draining and exhausting at times. It is important to know when God is talking to you. I encourage you to get up early in the morning and have an uninterrupted quiet time. Give your day and your problems to God, and pray for energy for your day. Learn that God can expand your time, strength, and spiritual giftedness, if you humbly submit your life to him on a daily basis.

Therefore put on the full armor of God, so that when the day of evil comes, you may be able to stand your ground, and after you have done everything, to stand. Stand firm then, with the belt of truth buckled around your waist, with the breastplate of righteousness in place, and with your feet fitted with the readiness that comes from the gospel of

peace. In addition to all this, take up the shield of faith, with which you
can extinguish all the flaming arrows of the evil one. Take the helmet of
salvation and the sword of the Spirit, which is the word of God.
And pray in the Spirit on all occasions with all kinds of prayers and
requests. With this in mind, be alert and always keep on
praying for all the saints. Ephesians 6:13–18

17. Focus, focus, focus – It will be important for you as a leader to learn the skill of setting your priorities. This is the skill of focused time management and learning how to set tasks in priority of importance, or scheduling blocks of time to do needed tasks. Learn to block out noise, set aside specific hours of your day and areas of your life, so you will have time to manage your day better, with God's help. Pray for God to allow you to focus effectively on your small group duties, weekly study, ministry administration paperwork, family, children, everyday job, or whatever might be in front of you. If we learn this valuable skill of a prayer-based focus, this powerful focused energy can be very productive as God uses you.

I press on to take hold of that for which Christ Jesus took hold of me.
Philippians 3:12

A noble man makes noble plans, and by noble deeds he stands.
Isaiah 32:8

Blessed is the man who does not condemn himself by what he approves.
Romans 14:22

18. Set goals for yourself and your ministry – It's important for you to have written goals for your ministry, for yourself personally, and for your family. If you don't write them down, most likely you will not accomplish your goals. On the flip side, if you write them down you will most likely accomplish your goals. Ask yourself and ask God to show you: "Why on Earth am I here?" The answer to this question will help you set goals that are consistent with God's plans for you.

I challenge you to pray and ask God to show you his purpose for you. Ask God why he created you. When you make this your goal, you're on your way to healthy reasoning and you begin learning God's purpose for your life. I encourage you to read *The Purpose Driven Life* by Dr. Rick Warren (Zondervan). You can learn the easy way or the hard way. One of

the first things to know is that there are no accidents in life. God designed it all. Colossians 1:16 (Msg) says: *For everything, absolutely everything, above and below, visible and invisible, rank after rank after rank of angels— everything got started in him and finds its purpose in him.*

God's desire is for you to grow into the person he created you to be. It begins at birth and continues throughout our lives; it's a process. The season you are in right now is part of that process.

> You can learn the easy way or the hard way...
> and one of the first things to know is that there are no accidents.

God refines you in the midst of your crisis. *See, I have refined you, though not as silver; I have tested you in the furnace of affliction* (Isaiah 48:10). He reworks the rough edges and polishes off your shortcomings and your dysfunctions through pain, so that you can be used for his glory in a future season. God never wastes a hurt and he does not waste your pain. If your heart and your mind are open to what he is about in your life, you will soon discover that there are no accidents. Our lives are part of a grand design.

It's important for you to have written goals for your ministry.

Ask yourself: **Why on Earth am I here?**

<u>Goals to list:</u>

(Please put out extra paper to list and reflect on these important goals for your life.)

1) What do I hope to accomplish in my ministry in the next year?

2) What do I want to accomplish in my ministry in the next 5 years?

3) What are my life purposes?

4) How can I use my gifts and talents to glorify God?

> *I consider my life worth nothing to me, if only I may finish the race and complete the task the Lord Jesus has given me—the task of testifying to the gospel of God's grace.* Acts 20:24

19. Integrity, integrity, integrity – It is important to have integrity in your group and ministry. Try to hear God, having integrity in your actions and words in your small group and your life. Without a clear sense of integrity in your small group, your group will not get very far. Rather, on the flip side, if you have integrity in your ministry, your group will grow and thrive. You will be highly respected as a person of integrity, which is very rare in today's society. God's words are clear in the book of Philippians, chapter 4:

> *Finally, brothers whatever is true, whatever is noble, whatever is*
> *right, whatever is pure, whatever is lovely, whatever is admirable—*
> *if anything is excellent or praiseworthy—think about such things.*
> *Whatever you have learned or received or heard from me, or seen*
> *in me—put it in practice, and the God of peace will be with you.*
> Philippians 4:8–9

Without a clear sense of integrity in your small group,
your group will not get very far.

20. Have guidelines of high moral standards in leadership – It is important to follow these simple guidelines so that you do not place yourself in a compromising position. Learn that the key is to be accountable to Godly people around you. Know that you need other strong Godly people around you (and they need you) to help keep you on God's pathway. Learn to be disciplined and to avoid situations that may be seen as compromising. Do not say (as so many which have gone before you and fallen) "It will never happen to me!" Know that Satan is the master of deception and will start with practical truths to get you to rationalize an area in your life that you should not. A little seed is planted in your mind and you follow this by compromising an area of your life. A simple definition of a rationalization is *a rational lie*. The world famous evangelist of our time, Dr. Billy Graham, had a list of high standards for himself and his staff of leaders. A similar list of key guidelines follows:

Do not say
"It will never
happen to
me!"

Guidelines for Small Group Leadership

1. There must be no visiting someone of the opposite sex in their home. Even if both are single.

2. Never counsel the opposite sex; find someone of the same sex to counsel them.

3. There should be no meetings or any activities alone with the opposite sex. Even if both are single.

4. Do not show affection of any kind to the opposite sex.

5. Do not discuss relationship problems with the opposite sex. Instead, refer them to a counselor of their same sex.

6. Do not discuss sexual problems with the opposite sex. Instead, refer them to a counselor of their same sex.

7. Do not answer cards, emails, or letters from the opposite sex.

8. Be guarded with physical closeness with group members of the opposite sex.

9. Pray for integrity for yourself and other small group leaders.

Above all else, guard your heart, for it is the wellspring of life. Put away perversity from your mouth; keep corrupt talk far from your lips. Let your eyes look straight ahead, fix your gaze directly before you. Make level paths for your feet and only take ways that are firm. Do not swerve to the right or the left; keep your foot from evil.
Proverbs 4:23–27

Search me, O God, and know my heart; test me and know my anxious thoughts. See if there is any offensive way in me, and lead me in the way everlasting. Psalm 139:23–24

Teaching Skills

21. Surround yourself with other wise leaders – Two, three, four, or more heads are wiser than one. Wisdom breeds still more wisdom. Bring problems and issues to your respected leaders, pastors, lay leaders, or counselors so you can make decisions based on Godly principles and input.

> **Remember, God is not the master of confusion; Satan is.**

Remember, God is not the master of confusion; Satan is the master of confusion and deception.

> *Instruct a wise man and he will be wiser still; teach a righteous man and he will add to his learning.* Proverbs 9:9

> *Nevertheless, the righteous will hold to their ways, and those with clean hands will grow stronger.* Job 17:9

22. Prayer preparation of leaders prior to the group meeting – The time just before a group meeting is a very important time of group leadership. This is where you and your fellow leaders prayerfully prepare yourselves by meeting prior to the start of each group meeting to pray. Plan to meet for a minimum of thirty minutes, to as much as sixty minutes, for set up and prayer prior to the group meeting starting. This is based on your set up time and preparation that is needed. This also is time where you unwind from your work day, discuss the group agenda, and pray to be God's powerful vessels. Pray that those hurting and in need will attend, and that their hearts will be open and receptive. Pray that you can be *"God with skin on"* to impact your group in a mighty way. It is far better to be early rather than late, prepared with your armor of the Holy Spirit as you lead in his power!

> Pray that you can be *"God with skin on"* to impact your group.

> *I pray that out of his glorious riches he may strengthen you with power through his Spirit in your inner being, so that Christ may dwell in your hearts through faith.* Ephesians 3:16–17

23. Real life-style teaching – Share from your heart. Make your words real, honest, and genuine words of God. If the members cannot relate to you, they will not gain as much from you. Maybe you might share real life stories about yourself, your struggles, your hurts, hang-ups, and shortcomings. This is where you're a transparent leader and your group can feel your honest, genuine leadership. With God's guidance, your teaching becomes real "mashed potatoes and gravy style" lessons in life, helping to change those you touch in your group.

I have filled him with the Spirit of God, with skill, ability,
and knowledge in all kinds of crafts. Exodus 31:3

If group members cannot relate to you,
they will not gain as much from you.

24. Servant leadership – Jesus Christ is the master leader and model servant leader. We should observe and study his servant-like qualities. Suggested books to study are *The Master Plan of Evangelism* by Robert E. Coleman or *My Utmost For His Highest* by Oswald Chambers. Learn how to be an effective servant leader, leading others by example, showing traits of meekness, humility and grace as Jesus Christ modeled for us.

Whoever wants to become great among you must be your servant,
and whoever wants to be first must be slave of all. For even the
Son of Man did not come to be served, but to serve, and to give his life
as a ransom for many. Mark 10:43–45

That joy is mine, and it is now complete. He must
become greater; I must become less. John 3:29–30

25. Strive to stay in the "God zone" – Stay out of any conflicts in your group or ministry, focusing only on what God wants for you and your ministry. Learn to have pure motives in your ministry. Put your ego in your back pocket, so you can have a clean and pure agenda in the "God zone." This is where there is a clear focus on God. You are clearly a vessel to be used by God, for his purpose. Learn to hear God and stay under his umbrella.

I consider everything a loss compared to the surpassing greatness of knowing Christ Jesus my Lord, for whose sake I have lost all things. I consider them rubbish, that I may gain Christ. Philippians 3:8

Learn to work for an audience of "One," and that is God.

26.   Leading for an audience of "One" in ministry – God is the CEO of our ministry. Yes, you will need to submit to the church, or the church board, or report to a pastor in charge of your small group. Learn to stay under God's wing, under his umbrella, and stay out of the politics of the church. Learn to work for an audience of "One," and that is God. We should respond as Jesus Christ would have responded, and take action as he would have. Learn to ask yourself: "What would Jesus do?" Follow Jesus Christ's guidance, and your leadership skills, with a discerning spirit, will get stronger. By doing this, you will increase in wisdom as a leader.

Whoever can be trusted with very little can be trusted with much, and whoever is dishonest with very little will also be dishonest with much. So if you have not been trustworthy in handling worldly wealth, who will trust you with true riches? And if you have not been trustworthy with someone else's property, who will give property of your own?
Luke 16:10–12

27. Know that God ultimately picks the leaders – God knows every hair on your head. He knew you before you were born. He knows which leaders can be effective. He knows the potential you can have as a leader for him, if you allow him to lead you. In regards to considering new leaders, most potential leaders are already leading before they acquire an official title. Learn to follow where God is leading and directing. Pray, listen, and wait to see what God may or may not be saying through other potential leaders, including those which you may be considering for your leadership team.

By their fruit you will recognize them. Do people pick grapes from thorn bushes, or figs from thistles? Likewise every good tree bears good fruit, but a bad tree bears bad fruit. A good tree cannot bear bad fruit, and a bad tree cannot bear good fruit. Every tree that does not bear good fruit is cut down and thrown into the fire. Thus by their fruit you will recognize them. Matthew 7:16–20

Regarding your leadership team, remember:
"By their fruit you will recognize them."

28. If you're not sure what to do, wait on the Lord! – *God is not the author of confusion* (1 Cor. 14:33 KJV). As we mentioned previously, Satan is the master of lies and deception. If you are not sure where God is in the situation, wait until you are clear as to what God is saying, or what he wants you to do. Pray for his wisdom or Godly advice. Surrender the situation to him before you move forward. A suggestion is to ask for advice and input from three to four other respected and discerning Godly people around you. If their advice is very similar, this is usually the correct answer. A poor decision in your group, or choosing the wrong assistant leader, can cause more damage in the long run than you can imagine.

Being strengthened with all power according to the Lord's glorious might so that you may have great endurance and patience. Job 26:14

29. Mentoring others and being mentored by others – Paul, who wrote a good portion of the New Testament, mentored Timothy, who was very young and had a lot to learn, but was a great man of God. Paul, on the other hand, was mentored by Barnabas in his early years of ministry. So, as shown by example: we also need to be sandwiched between being taught, and at the same time, teaching and mentoring others. It is best for you as leader to be in your own personal group with other group leaders that are not necessarily looking to you to lead them or the group. Rather, you are a trusted and accountable group member. Your own personal group, where you learn and grow, being challenged to *be all that you can be!* (If you lead a small group, or a support group or other group, in a leadership capacity, it is important that you have your own separate small group of a trusted few. This is so you can have a safe place to share and grow, in a confidential manner.)

*This is a trustworthy saying. And I want you to stress these things,
so that those who have trusted in God may be careful to
devote themselves to doing what is good. These things are
excellent and profitable for everyone.* Titus 3:8

30. Use humor in your groups – Group members do not listen to leaders and group members they do not like. Be a good storyteller, using humor to make a key point. You might use clean, simple, short story humor about yourself, or other things that come to mind, to drive your point across. Jesus Christ was very creative. He used humor and taught with what he had, and so can *you*!

*Be imitators of God, therefore, as dearly loved children and live a life
of love, just as Christ loved us and gave himself up for us as a fragrant
offering and sacrifice to God.* Ephesians 5:1–2

31. Timing is very important – Know that God's timing is always perfect and never late! God is never early, God is never late! Timing is important in leadership and in making good decisions at the right time. Timing can also be important in helping a person that's hurting and needs to ponder and give more thought to an issue. Good timing in explaining a point can help a group member see God's point clearer. Yet sometimes you may need to wait, if someone is not ready to hear something or they have a hardened heart. Sometimes a person in front of you could be rationalizing an area of their life and not receptive to what God wants to tell them at that moment. Wait on the timing of the Holy Spirit, learning to make better decisions, or sharing with others with better timing, or use discerning words with better timing. Learn to wait on God's timing and become a better leader as God uses you.

> **Wait on the timing of the Holy Spirit,
> learning to make better decisions.**

*Do your best to present yourself to God as one approved,
a workman who does not need to be ashamed and who correctly
handles the word of truth.* 2 Timothy 2:15

Seek the Lord while he may be found; call on him while he is near. Let the wicked forsake his way and the evil man his thoughts. Let him turn to the Lord, and he will have mercy on him, and to our God, for he will freely pardon. Isaiah 55:6–7

32. Ministry is a heart condition – Ministry is all about service to others, the right humble teaching heart, and having a *servant-like* attitude and qualities. If your heart is in the right place and you genuinely care about your group, you'll lead with a prayerful humble discerning spirit. Learn to start your days on your knees, praying to have a humble servant-like attitude and your ministry and group will go far. A poor heart condition can be a stumbling block in ministry, in your group, in your family, at work, or any area of your life. Ask God if you have unresolved *heart problems* in your life. Challenge God to gently put your poor heart condition into proper perspective, helping you learn to deal with the challenging areas of your life. Remember that if you have any resentment, bitterness, or non-transparent sinful areas in your life, these issues can be harmful to your group and ministry, blocking gifts or blessings in your life which God has set aside for you. Think about it!

The goal of this is love, which comes from a pure heart and a good conscience and a sincere faith. Some have wandered away from these and turned to meaningless talk. They want to be teachers of the law, but they do not know what they are taking about or what they so confidently affirm. 1 Timothy 1:5–7

Challenge God to gently put your poor heart condition into proper perspective.

33. Delegating and team teaching – Another important tool is team teaching, which helps take the pressure off one person doing the group study every week. To the degree possible, **delegate the weekly study to others, sometimes even if they are not an official leader.** This is a way to develop a potential leader. Another idea is to **co-lead when someone has a powerful testimony, letting other group members have an opportunity to learn and grow.** If you do a study, prepare well in advance. When you do teach, you, the facilitator, quite often are the one who learns the most since you are the person preparing the study. Prepare with a clean heart and a clear agenda.

This will allow God to use you to impact his kingdom, even with a short 15 to 30 minute study. In your teaching, **mix up the four learning styles: a) Visual techniques, b) Writing techniques, c) Group participation with challenging questions, and d) Listening techniques** (see item #35). All of these items are based on a wonderful tape series by Bruce H. Wilkerson called *Teaching with Style)*. Each of your group members learns differently, and by using teaching methods that apply to the different learning styles, you will keep your small group on their toes, alert, and learning. For example, you might consider doing little skits or little short visual studies.

Remember, you are just the vessel.
Your job is to be available and God will use *you!*

Listen, for I have worthy things to say; I open my lips to speak what is right. My mouth speaks what is true, for my lips detest wickedness. All the words of my mouth are just; none of them is crooked or perverse. To the discerning all of them are right; they are faultless to those who have knowledge. Proverbs 8:6–9

34. A good leader makes room for others to lead – A good leader knows how to step aside to let others lead, let others grow, let others mature, let others shine for God's glory. Something to consider: if you are always leading, always talking, maybe, just maybe, you might come across as controlling to those in front of you. Ask God to give you wisdom and discernment so you can find a balance in teaching, learning to step aside at times to allow others to lead. This will also help others to learn and grow into leaders, as Jesus Christ did.

Do you see a man skilled in his work? He will serve before kings; he will not serve before obscure men. Proverbs 21:5

Find a balance in teaching, learning to
step aside at times to allow others to lead.

As iron sharpens iron, so one man sharpens another. Proverbs 27:17

35. Vary your teaching styles – Jesus Christ was our Master Teacher. He taught us through story telling, while using four different teaching methods as he walked on this Earth. In your Bible you will see many, many examples of parables in the books of Matthew, Mark, Luke, and John. Bruce H. Wilkerson has several series of tapes and one very good series is called *Teaching With Style,* which shows some of Jesus Christ's teaching styles. Some different teaching styles include:

a) **Visual techniques** – Illustrate points to your group with charts, skits, or writing boards. Use these to allow God's words to come alive visually.

b) **Writing methods** – Create your group studies and handouts with blanks to fill in. Some group members will learn better when they write down answers and take notes to remind them of the key points. Learn to create open-ended questions to help your group think.

c) **Group participation** – Ask the group for their feedback verbally, including their feelings, opinions, or ideas about what is being discussed. This is important to do during a study, as it helps members to stay focused on the discussion topic, and it usually raises questions that other members may also have. This will help you as a leader to identify what is important to the group. Be careful that you don't stray too far from the prepared study. It's very simple to do a follow-up study if there are a number of questions raised about the subject, and you run out of time to discuss them.

**Learn to keep the attention of the group while you
move around the room, varying the tone of your voice.**

d) **Listening** – Learn to keep the attention of the group while you move around the room, varying the tone of your voice. Ask a question of a person who does not appear to be listening. Keep the pace of your group moving and group members will be excited to participate and learn. This will help keep the group alert.

Each person in your group will learn differently. By mixing up the learning styles, you can reach each member in a manner which they can learn the best.

*If you hold to my teaching, you are really my disciples. Then you will
know the truth, and the truth will set you free.* John 8:31

Be strong in the Lord and in his mighty power. Ephesians 6:10

I can do everything through Christ who strengthens me.
Philippians 4:13 (GW)

36. Prepare a weekly study and handout with blanks to be completed –
It is a valuable teaching tool to have a short study of fifteen to thirty minutes
to begin your group meeting. It offers the group something to think about,
to reflect upon, and can challenge them to grow. Start preparing by inviting
the power of the Holy Spirit, asking God to help you with your presentation.
It is important that it is quiet and you are alone with God, for him to speak
to you, in your preparation of the study. Develop a study and pray God will
open hearts and minds to receive his message through you. As thoughts come
to you during the week, take notes for your weekly study, learning the value of
early prayers, asking for God's help in your study, preparation, and delivery.

*...guard my teachings as the apple of your eye. Bind them on your
fingers; write them on the tablet of your heart.* Proverbs 7:2–3

37. After a short study, break into sharing groups – A general sequence
for a small group meeting can be:

a) Open the meeting in prayer, inviting the Holy Spirit to your small
group (groups) with transparency.

b) State any announcements quickly to keep the meeting moving.

c) Have a fifteen- to thirty-minute study time for the group to learn and
grow, based on time available. It is important to not have the lesson too long,
leaving the overall group hungry for more of God's word. Learn to follow the
guidance of the Holy Spirit and be flexible in the group study time; you may
want to make changes in your teaching based on topic and group questions.

> **Learn to follow the guidance of the Holy Spirit
> and be flexible in the group**

d) Quickly break into four- to six-person round-table sharing groups,
based on the size of your overall group.

e) Have each round table group share separately at their tables. Each table group should end their meeting in prayer, or you can end with prayer as an overall group together.

f) Encourage group members to connect throughout the week, as this is a form of accountably and encouragement from the group.

> ...if any of you on Earth agree about anything you ask for, it will be done for you by my Father in heaven. For where two or three come together in my name, there am I with them. Matthew 18:19–20

Using short skits or visual methods to illustrate a point, is a powerful way to express a key point to your group.

38. Use visuals in your group study – Using short skits or visual methods to illustrate a point, is a powerful way to express a key point to your group. One example of visual teaching can be an example of how words or an expressed tone of our voice can be harmful in relationships. Use a large cardboard box lid and a pair of scissors to demonstrate this point. As you are talking to the group, punch holes in the cardboard box lid with a pair of scissors. This simple skit, which illustrates the damage of inappropriate tone or hurtful words, which when spoken to others, can affect their self-esteem for years. In a symbolic way, even if you were to patch the holes in the box (a person's life), it's still a patch or repair. Damaging words cannot be taken back. A person could go to counseling for years afterwards, trying to let go of the damaging words implanted in their mind.

A second group visual example is: when you're trying to get your group to understand and hear God better, a simple visual example is to shut off the lights in your room during the middle of your study. Use this as an example to listen to the darkness. Show your group this simple visual example, stopping the group, trying to hear the silence, trying to hear what God might be telling them. Leave the small group room lights off for a couple minutes, whispering God's words, driving home this simple visual example. Encourage your group to listen to the Holy Spirit in their daily quiet time or in a challenging season of life. What is God saying, or the darkness saying, to you or a group member? Often your daily quiet time is the most valuable time of the day. Learn that silence and darkness can be very valuable and expressive tools to use in your group teaching. Try something similar to these examples and you might be surprised how a simple, creative visualization can impact the group. This is especially effective for men who are very visual in their learning abilities.

Instruct a wise man and he will be wiser still; teach a righteous man and he will add to his learning. Proverbs 9:9

39. Use testimonies in your group study – From time to time, use testimonies in your study time as another powerful learning tool. Ask a group member to share their personal journey in life, expressing their struggles and challenges. This can be a powerful demonstration of how God transformed their heart and mind. Group members will see that there is hope in what God can do in their lives.

Do not let your heart envy sinners, but always be zealous for the fear of the Lord. There is surely a future hope for you, and your hope will not be cut off. Proverbs 23:17–18

Teamwork

40. Have mentorship by leaders available to group members – Learn that to spend time mentoring others is a very valuable key to leadership. Sometimes you might spend more time with a certain group member, knowing a group member is processing an issue, and spending time with him can help keep him out of trouble, grow in the process, and learn to make better decisions. A group member needs to know that his leaders care and what a Godly person looks like. How a group leader acts or responds can affect a group member for eternity. Every group member is a potential leader, and developing, teaching, and spending time with them can help them see that they too can be used by God to help others.

Think how you have instructed many, how you have strengthened feeble hands. Your words have supported those who stumbled; you have strengthened faltering knees. Job 4:3–4

**How a group leader acts or responds
can affect a group member for eternity.**

41. Delegate duties to group members – Learn the valuable skill of delegating group tasks to others. Items to delegate might include: maintaining the phone list, keeping attendance, rotating the weekly studies to other potential leaders, opening or closing the group meeting in prayer, setting up the study room, or making phone calls to help connect new group members. Delegating also makes your job as a group leader much easier, and allows your group members to become an integral part of their group.

*All authority in heaven and on Earth has been given to me. Therefore
go and make disciples...and teaching them to obey everything I have
commanded you.* Matthew 28:18–20

42. Obey God – Pray for wisdom and discernment as you lead your group: learning to listen and follow the guidance of the Holy Spirit. Most likely you will have to pinch yourself from time to time as you follow the Holy Spirit. Learn to be obedient to wherever the Holy Spirit may be leading you.

*You are awesome, O God, in your sanctuary; the
God of Israel give power and strength to his people.
Praise be to God!* Psalm 68:35

**Have God
check your eyes,
your mouth, and
your attitude.**

43. Challenge God to clean up your act – Do a periodic checkup with God, praying to have God search you for the things in your life and personality that you need to work on. God wants to use you as a clean vessel. Pray to have God check your eyes, your mouth, your attitude, your spending habits, your personality shortcomings, or other areas of your life. If you are truly honest, you will have a list of areas in your life which can be improved on, with God's help!

Search me, O God, and know my heart; test me and know
my anxious thoughts. See if there is any offensive way in me,
and lead me in the way everlasting. Psalm 139:23

44. Balance family and ministry – Family priorities need to come first. If you have issues at home or problems with your spouse, your home life needs to take a priority over your role as a small group leader. It is important for your spouse and children to be on the same page with you in your group leadership and ministry. If you do not have their full support, you should think carefully about not leading a group or being involved in a church ministry away from home. This can add to stresses which all ready exist, and not be in your family's best interest. Satan can do more damage, if he tears a part a leader's family, not to mention how many eyes are watching your personal life.

But you, man of God…pursue righteousness, godliness, faith, love,
endurance and gentleness. Fight the good fight of the faith. Take hold
of the eternal life to which you were called when you make your good
confession in the presence of many witnesses. In the sight of God, who
gives life to everything,…keep this command without spot or blame
until the appearing of our Lord Jesus Christ… 1 Timothy 6:11–14

45. Ministry is a sacrifice – You will learn that ministry is a sacrifice of time, money, family, sleep, energy, friends, or many other things. Pray to God that you will make the most of your energy, family time, and work time. God can stretch and expand you in all areas, to accomplish his purpose(s). Know that God can be extremely creative to meet his goals, in his timing. Just know that God is never early, or never too late, His timing is always perfect!

> **Ministry is a sacrifice of time, money, family, sleep,**
> **energy, friends, or many other things.**

Be diligent in these matters; give yourself wholly to them,
so that everyone may see your progress. Watch your life and doctrine
closely. Persevere in them, because if you do, you will save
both yourself and your hearers. 1 Timothy 4:15–16

46. Surrender control to God's ministry – Because it is ultimately God's ministry, to be effective, know that he is in control and you must be proactive with him. Submit to his leading and surrender to his plans for your life and ministry. When we forget this important truth, and do not listen or submit to God's guidance, we can get into trouble very quickly. Learn to stay under God's umbrella, having a humble attitude and earnestly try to hear God's voice, where he provides all our needs in life and ministry. Stay as a player on God's ball field, at any position he wants you to play on his team. Let go of control, and your ministry will flourish and grow!

Do your best to present yourself to God as one approved, a workman who does not need to be ashamed and who correctly handles the word of truth. Avoid godless chatter, because those who indulge in it will become more and more ungodly. Their teaching will become spread like gangrene. 2 Timothy 2:15–17

It is important to have a passion for your God-given ministry.

47. Have a passion for your ministry and your group – It is important to have a passion for your God-given ministry and group. If you are not 100 percent sold out to your church, your ministry, and your group, you will need to think twice about being involved in it. Ministry can be very demanding, but extremely rewarding for those passionate about their God-given ministry and purpose.

However, I consider my life worth nothing to me, if only I may finish the race and complete the task the Lord Jesus has given me—the task of testifying to the gospel of God's grace. Acts 20:24

48. Study the master teacher – Studying how our greatest teacher, Jesus Christ, taught is very important to your leadership growth. Find books, podcasts, or video tapes which give instruction on teaching as Jesus did. Soon, your teaching methods and techniques will improve dramatically. A very good book to read and study about Jesus' teaching is: *The Master Plan of Evangelism,* by Robert E. Coleman. Also a wonderful tape series for leaders or those considering leadership is *Teaching With Style,* by Dr. Bruce Wilkerson.

The hardworking farmer should be the first to receive a share of crops. Reflect on what I am saying, for the Lord will give you insight into all this. 2 Timothy 2:6–7

How our greatest teacher, Jesus Christ, taught is very important to your leadership growth.

49. If you need help: ask, seek, and knock – In ministry, don't be afraid to ask for help from God, or from your group, or from your church. Pray and God will place the help or resources that you need right in front of you. If at all possible, lean toward your small group taking care of their own needs. Try to not be a high-maintenance group, or a burden to the church body. Most churches run on very lean budgets, and pastors or staff members are already stretched very thin for time and resources. Since God promises to provide our needs, know that he will not let your group down.

Lean toward your small group taking care of their own needs.

Ask and it will be given to you; seek and you will find; knock and the door will be opened to you. For everyone who asks receives; he who seeks finds; and to him who knocks, the door will be opened. Matthew 7:7–8

50. Choose co-leaders very carefully – A simple and great way to learn more about a potential co-leader is to visit their home. By interacting with them in a casual setting, you can observe how they function away from the group, seeing their priorities in life, and how they live. By interacting with them away from a church setting you might be surprised what you can learn about a potential leader in a few minutes. If you are not sure about a leader, error on the side of caution, as a poor co-leader can do a lot of damage quickly.

*If anyone sets his heart on being an overseer, he desires a noble task.
Now the overseer must be above reproach, the husband of but one wife,
temperate, self-controlled, respectful, hospitable, able to teach, not given
to drunkenness, not violent but gentle, not quarrelsome, not a lover of
money. He must manage his own family well and see that his children
obey him with proper respect. (If anyone does not know how to manage
his own family, how can he take care of God's church?) He must not
be a recent convert, or he may become conceited and fall under the
same judgment of the devil. He must have a good reputation with
outsiders, so that he will not fall into disgrace and into the devil's trap.*
1 Timothy 3:1–7

Getting Started

As we close this section, pray day after day, for God to open doors and
put on your heart a clear direction. Ask him to show you a clear pathway for
your group and ministry and to guide you, as you share and mentor others,
impacting them for eternity.

II. LEADERSHIP CHARACTERISTICS FOR A HEALTHY SMALL GROUP

Many of the leadership qualities you learn from your ministry team of leaders also apply when you lead small group meetings. In a sense, this is where the "rubber meets the road." In small group meetings God can, and will, use you to help hurting group members and to help teach them what he has for them to learn. As you'll see in the following paragraphs, there are many keys to leading and teaching your small group members and building a sense of teamwork, connection, and support between the group members.

Functions and Responsibilities

51. Bonding in crisis – This is where God does his best work, in the midst of a crisis, helping us face our challenges head on. Rally around hurting members of your small group. They could be emotionally bleeding badly and have a need to share. A good leader should model the skills of empathizing, listening, and asking good questions to get a hurting member to think. Example questions you might ask a group member are: What does God want you to learn? What is your part in this crisis you are dealing with? How can you begin to work on the issue or issues before you?

> *Consider it pure joy, my brothers, whenever you face trials of many kinds, because you know that the testing of your faith develops perseverance. Perseverance must finish its work so that you may be mature and complete, not lacking anything.* James 1:2–3

52. Encourage a war-like bond of fellowship in your group – The situation in your group is similar to army buddies that lift each other up, protecting each other on the right and on the left. It is this "band-of-brothers" attitude that helps encourage and mold group members into Godly examples.

But encourage one another daily, as long as it is called Today, so that none of you may be hardened by sin's deceitfulness. Hebrews 3:13

53. Being accountable to the group – Accountability with love is important in a group. Group members or a new member might be earnestly trying to learn new habits and learn Godly ways, so it is very important that group members lovingly help keep each other focused on God. Accountability is needed for all of us, as anyone can slip and fall very easily. Encourage group accountability, since none of us is above slipping, especially when we have to go it alone.

> **Accountability is needed for all of us, as anyone can slip and fall very easily.**

He who trusts in himself is a fool, but he who walks in wisdom is kept safe. Proverbs 28:26

An anxious heart weighs a man down, but a kind word cheers him up. Proverbs 12:25

54. Having social activities with accountability – Group social activities with a light form of accountability can be very helpful to connect and bond the group in a casual environment. Examples of social activities are a pizza night, movie night once a month, or going to a retreat or seminar together as a group. You might also ask someone to meet new group members for coffee after a church service. Learning the gift of hospitality and modeling accountability in social settings is key to helping group members grow.

God, who has you into fellowship with his son Jesus Christ our Lord, is faithful. 1 Corinthians 1:9

55. "Work on me, work on me, work on me!" – Encourage your members to work on their own issues. A great question to ask might be: "What would your wife (or husband) or family members say you need to work on?" Learn to ask your group good questions, challenging them to think and grow. Another question to ask is: "What can you do this week to start making a difference to change tomorrow?" Changing tomorrow does not start with the major changes in a person's life, rather changing tomorrow starts with God's help and the little *baby steps* which are taken day-by-day, little-by-little. As a leader, learn and share that we can do nothing to change others in life; we can only choose to work on our own issues and shortcomings. This key central theme needs to be modeled, beginning with group leaders. Your group members will soon absorb and follow by working on their own issues.

> Changing tomorrow starts with God's help and the little
> *baby steps* which are taken day-by-day, little-by-little.

Commit to the Lord whatever you do, and your plans will succeed.
Proverbs 16:3

I am the Lord, the God of all mankind. Is anything too hard for me?
Jeremiah 32:27

56. Model studying God's Word – If anyone in your group is not reading the Bible or meditating on verses, it's a simple fact that they are not growing. Gently encourage and suggest ways that verses can be read, memorized, and absorbed, so your group members will grow.

All scripture is God-breathed and is useful for teaching, rebuking, correcting, and training in righteousness, so that the man of God may be thoroughly equipped for every good work. 2 Timothy 3:16

57. Encourage a daily quiet time – The most powerful time of a group member's day is their quiet time. This sets the tone of his day, the tone of his attitude, and the tone of his responses to people he interacts with. Encourage devoting fifteen minutes a day or more to reading, studying, and meditating on God's word.

*The Lord gives strength to his people; the
Lord blesses his people with peace.* Psalm 29:11

He gives strength to the weary and increases the power of the weak.
Isaiah 40:29

58. Tools for the toolbox; memorizing Bible verses – Bible verses are God's tools given to his children. Encourage your group members to put tools in their toolbox by memorizing God's words, and incorporating them into their daily lifestyle. Challenge your group to start with short verses and to memorize one verse per week. These verses will be tools in their toolboxes. God's word stimulates our minds as a verse is memorized. Yes, this is part of God's plan when you memorize verses. Your mind is stimulated, and you gain wisdom and discernment as a result.

> *For the word of God is living and active. Sharper than any double-edged sword, it penetrates even to dividing soul and spirit, joints and marrow; it judges the thoughts and attitudes of the heart.*
> Hebrews 4:12

**Memory verses will be tools in your toolbox.
God's word stimulates our minds.**

59. Challenge group members to model Godly examples – Group members can be very susceptible to change. It is important for all group members to model Godly values in their words and actions. Over a period of weeks and months, each new group member in turn can see and show others what proper conduct is and the benefits that come from it.

> *In everything set them an example by doing what is good. In your teaching show integrity, seriousness and soundness of speech that cannot be condemned, so that those who oppose you may be ashamed because they have nothing bad to say about us.* Titus 2:7–8

Leadership Skills

60. Potter and clay (moldable) character – It is important to be flexible, moldable by God, and to attempt to live with a God-like character. Learn to be flexible in your group, as every week is different. Learn to follow the leading of the Holy Spirit in your small group. Jesus looked at them and said, *"With man this is impossible, but with God all things are possible"* (Matthew 19:36).

61. Ask good questions in the group – "Good" questions encourage group members to share without making them uncomfortable. "Good" questions also illicit more than a one-word answer, facilitate deeper sharing, and generate dialog among group members. Become a master of asking good questions, or in a lot of cases, be a "double-question" asker; ask follow-up questions to encourage deeper sharing. You may say "How are you doing?" Most will answer "fine" or "good." Then say "Tell me about 'fine' or 'good.'" Dig deeper and go under the surface. Ask open-ended questions to help your group member think and respond with more thoughtful answers to your questions. Hopefully, as a group member begins to trust the group and group leaders better, his (or her) answers will get to the real true feelings under their external masks or superficial personality.

> **Become a master of asking good questions, or,
> in a lot of cases, be a "double-question" asker;
> ask follow-up questions to encourage deeper sharing.**

Surely you heard of him and were taught in him in accordance with the truth that is in Jesus. You were taught, with regard to your former way of life... Ephesians 4:21

As for me, I am filled with power, and with justice and might.
Micah 3:8

62. Have a humble, teachable spirit – It is very important to have a humble spirit which God can use for his glory. Just about the time you believe how great you are, you can easily fail. If you stay on your knees, and remain humble and useable, God can change the areas in life in which you are weak. He will make you stronger than you could ever image in these same areas of your life. It is important to face your fears, knowing that only God can make you a strong and powerful instrument for his glory. Be willing to do whatever God asks of you to do, stepping out in faith!

My grace is sufficient for your, for my power is made perfect in weakness. Therefore I will boast all the more gladly about my weaknesses, so that Christ's power may rest on me. That is why, for Christ's sake, I delight in weaknesses, in insults, in hardships, in persecutions, in difficulties. For when I am weak, then I am strong.
2 Corinthians 12:9–10

**God can change the areas in life in which you are weak.
He will make you stronger.**

63. Have high moral standards for yourself and for group members – Group members will absorb what they see; similar to a dry sponge becoming filled with water. Help them fill up with living water. It is extremely important that group members have leaders whose lives are as pure and clean as possible, since a lot of eyes are watching a leader's actions. You will observe new members quoting you and doing what you do. Raise your level of integrity and the moral bar for yourself, thus modeling a Godly example for your fellow leaders and your group.

*Be careful that you do not forget the Lord your God, failing to observe
his commands, his laws and his decrees that I am giving you this day.*
Deuteronomy 8:11

64. Empathize with your group member's pain and needs – If you cannot taste, smell, or feel other's pain, you will most likely not be helpful to those you interact with. In most instances, an effective support group leader or small group leader has walked the path that group members are experiencing. If you are a leader, your job includes being a good listener, trying to hear a member's struggles or challenges.

**If you cannot taste, smell, or feel other's pain,
you will most likely not be helpful to those you interact with.**

*And we rejoice in the hope of the glory of God. Not only so, but we
rejoice in our sufferings, because we know that suffering produces
perseverance; perseverance, character; and character, hope. And hope
does not disappoint us, because God has poured out his love into our
hearts by the Holy Spirit, whom he has given us.* Romans 6:2–5

65. Develop the best small group possible – Pray continually for your group and for your group members. Encourage group members to pray for each other by allowing members to share their prayer requests and encouraging the use of the *Group Prayer Request* form. Learn to give God the credit for his ministry. You are just the caretaker of his group! Know when you do it God's way, your group can impact more members than you can dream possible. Stay humble, stay on your knees, modeling what a Godly leader is, and you will see God bless your group.

> *Then we will no longer be infants, tossed back and forth by the waves, and blown here and there by every wind of teaching and by the cunning and craftiness of men in their deceitful scheming. Instead, speaking the truth in love, we will in all things grow up into him who is the head, that is Christ. From him the whole body, joined and held together by every supporting ligament, grows and builds itself up in love, as each part does its work.* Ephesians 4:14–16

66. Have a creative, spontaneous small group – As a leader and teacher, your job is to prepare yourself well in advance of group starting time. With humble and powerful prayers, ask for God's help in your group. The Holy Spirit will give you a growing group that is also spontaneous and creative. You will need to have copies of the weekly prepared study or workbook outline for each group member. Start your study and ask challenging questions to get your group members to think. As you grow in confidence, you will learn to roll with your group's challenges, listening to God's discerning voice. Following what God may be saying requires trust, discipline, and obedience! You may be pinching yourself in the weeks and months to follow. Saying "WOW, did I really say that?" Pray over and over that God's wisdom and discernment will have an impact on your group. Learn that the Holy Spirit can fill you with spontaneous, creative wisdom and studies for the group.

As you grow in confidence, you will learn to roll with your group's challenges.

> *Think how you have instructed many, how you have strengthened feeble hands. Your words have supported those who stumbled; you have strengthened faltering knees.* Job 4:3–4

67. Share deeply with transparency – Your group will share as deep as their leader shares. If you share a deep personal story, so will your group members. On the flip side, if you are shallow in your presentation, your group may follow suit and also be very, very shallow. A group leadership technique to try is to share something personal about yourself that no one in the group knows. Ask that each person in the room also share. You may be surprised what might be shared by a group member who may have a deep-seated issue in his or her life. By uncovering an issue (such as previous emotional wound) a group member can grow or become unstuck. It is very, very important that the group be a safe place where group members can share from the heart. What is shared in a confidential manner must stay confidential. Talking behind someone's back and gossiping can be very harmful or destroy a group, like gangrene. A key to growth for you and your group is transparency, in a healthy and safe manner.

I am the light of the world. Whoever follows me will never walk in darkness, but will have the light of life. John 8:12

...pursue righteousness, faith, love and peace along with those who call on the Lord out of a pure heart. 2 Timothy 2:22

68. Be disciplined in knowing God better – It is important to be disciplined in studying and knowing God's word for you personally and for your ministry. Spend a minimum of thirty minutes to one hour each day, studying God's word. The more time you spend studying God's word, the more you will have a successful group and ministry. You may say you do not have enough time. Learn to pray for God to expand your time, your energy, and your resources. You may be surprised! Everything that you needed to get done in a day will get done! Know that God's timing is perfect. God can accomplish the desires of your heart and ministry, if you are focused on him. As you read below in John 15:5–9, you can see that if you are not plugged into God's word, fellowshiping with God's members, studying God's word day and night, so to speak, you will not be much good for God to use. Conversely, connected to God you can be a very productive vessel for him to use.

I am the vine; you are the branches. If a man remains in me and I in him, he will bear much fruit; apart from me you can do nothing. If anyone does not remain in me, he is like a branch that is thrown away and withers; such branches are picked up, thrown into the fire and burned. If you remain in me and my words remain in you, ask

whatever you wish, and it will be given you. This is to my Father's glory, that you bear much fruit, showing yourselves to be my disciples.
John 15:5–9

69. Know that with God's help, the weakest area in your life can become your greatest strength – The more honest, genuine, real, and transparent you are, God can increasingly use you in incredible ways. God wants us to be open and honest with him about all areas of our lives and shortcomings. He knows them anyway. If we let him, God can take the shortcomings in your marriage, your life, or the poor decisions of the past, and turn them into an incredible testimony for his glory.

Therefore, I will boast all the more gladly about my weakness, so that Christ's power may rest on me. That is why, for Christ's sake, I delight in weakness, in insults, in persecutions, in difficulties. For when I am weak, then I am strong. 2 Corinthians 12:9–10

Teaching Skills

70. Care of God's flock – Know your sheep, show your sheep, and grow your sheep! It is important to take care of the misdirected or lost "sheep" in your group. Encourage those in your group to follow the narrow path, and then mature the flock, with God's help. From time to time, you may need to check on one of your group members to see how they are really **Know your sheep, show your sheep, and grow your sheep!** doing. Often we can put on a hard outer shell of protection, or a sense that we have it all together, but often we can be hiding our real inner self, or hiding our wounded inner self. Express that you genuinely care and want the best for those in your group. Learn to share the love in your heart, as you care for those under your care. Pray for God to give guidance and the right words to encourage others to stay on God's pathway.

Those who hope in the Lord will renew their strength. They will soar on wings like eagles; they will run and not grow weary, they will walk and not be faint. Isaiah 40:31

71. Guard your heart and mind – It is impossible not to be tempted. Learn to guard your mind and heart so you will not set yourself up for failure. Feed your mind and heart with God's words. Learn to listen to praise and worship music, or verses, memorizing God's word and developing God-like thoughts to protect your mind throughout the day.

If your eye causes you to sin, pluck it out. It is better for you to enter the kingdom of God with one eye than to have two eyes and be thrown into hell. Mark 9:47

72. Hone in on the power of the Holy Spirit – This is where you prayerfully submit to the power of the Holy Spirit, humbling yourself in your daily quiet time, in your group meeting preparation time, and your prayer time before your small group meetings begin. You will learn firsthand that you will not get too far on your own power, you need the power of the Holy Spirit to be an effective leader. Learn to pray simple prayers throughout the day, or possibly a few minutes before the group meeting begins, asking for God's power and his Holy Spirit to guide you in your group and ministry. Use the incredible power of the Holy Spirit to make your job effective and easier.

When you are assembled in the name of our Lord Jesus...I am with you in spirit, and the power of our Lord Jesus is present. 1 Corinthians 5:4

73. Watch out for pride, issues, debating, or personality conflicts – A small group atmosphere is not a place for pride or ego issues, or debating unrelated issues that have no point to most members of the group. Make decisions based on what God's word teaches and what is best for the group. As we stated previously, Jesus Christ is not the master of confusion, Satan is, and he would love nothing better than to have your group start debating an unrelated issue in your group meeting. Another example is if one of the group members has a strong personality and wants to have the last word, debating a useless point and unrelated point. It is okay to call a time out and change the focus back to the study. Learn to focus on God in the situation! Ask yourself what would Jesus Christ do in the situation. What would your respected Pastor, or a respected godly friend say

Learn to focus on God in the situation!

or do? Learn to stay out of the gray areas, focusing on your study. Encourage unrelated discussions to be continued at a later time, after the group meeting is over.

We are therefore Christ's ambassadors, as though God were making his appeal through us. We implore you on Christ's behalf: Be reconciled to God. God made him who has no sin to be sin for us, so that in him we might become the righteousness of God. 2 Corinthians 5:20–21

74. Keep your group on their toes – Your best teachers in school kept you on the edge of your seat. Many times you did not know what the teacher was going to do and you learned a lot from them. With God's help, you can have eyes in the back of your head. Mix up what is done in the group, trying different things, challenging the group to learn and grow. As Jesus keeps us on our toes, keep your group curious and wondering what you are going to do next. Maybe do a simple visual skit, which can help express the message of your group, or listen to a tape related to your study for a few minutes, then open it up for group discussion. Mix up your teaching styles leaving your group hungry for more (See item 35 of this book: *Vary Your Teaching Styles.*), leaving your group hungry for more.

Let us hold unswervingly to the hope we profess, for he who promised is faithful. And let us consider how we may spur one another on toward love and good deeds. Hebrews 10:23–24

75. Group principles are based on godly principles – God's word should be your group's foundation, thus his words should be the final word. Pray a simple prayer; that God shows you the correct verse to use, which can express your point clearly. Try and give your group members simple concluding points from your study. Much of the time, life can be so complex and if we take away the gray areas in the situation, the real problem becomes clearer. Life's challenges can become much easier to understand, following the ways that God may be suggesting to resolve the situation.

Whatever is true, whatever is noble, whatever is right, whatever is pure, whatever is lovely, whatever is admirable—if anything is excellent or praiseworthy—think about such things. Philippians 4:8

76. Balance grace, truth, and love in your groups – It is important to follow the teachings of Jesus Christ. He modeled a balance between grace, truth, and love. With too much truth, you can be correct and emphasize a point too strongly, turning off a new member and coming across as excessively legalistic. You can make your point and lose the battle. Share with love in your heart, and a proper tone in the group, offering a lot of grace to new members. Lead similar to how Jesus Christ did, modeling an appropriate balance of grace, truth, and love.

If you hold to my teaching, you are really my disciples. Then you will know the truth, and the truth will set you free. John 8:31–32

77. Be real and down to Earth with group members – If your small group can't relate to you as a leader, you are little or no value to them. It is extremely important for you to be real, honest, and transparent, so others can see the God-like qualities within you. The flip side is that, if we use too much religious language, you can lose the group or a new member. Maybe a new member might be trying to figure out what this God stuff is all about. A new member needs to see that he can relate to a real human being, who is honest, genuine, and of a God-like character.

We are taking pains to do what is right, not only in the eyes of the Lord but also in the eyes of men. 2 Corinthians 8:21

78. Watch the body language of those in your group – As you lead your group, watch what your group members are doing around you, or how they are responding to your message. Somewhere around 86 to 93 percent of communication is non-verbal (Mehrabians' Communication Research Data and Professor Albert Mehrabia's book *Silent Messages*). Learn to "read" what your group members are saying *by their body language*. Is someone sleeping, or distracted in the corner? Does someone have their back to the speaker and sending a message on his cell phone? Is a group member gazing off into thin air? Keep your group members on their toes during your group meeting. Move around the room, do different things, mixing up the routine. Maybe ask a question of the person not paying attention or adjust your delivery to accommodate what your room is telling you. The more group experience you have, the more confident you will become. With God's help, you can become a very effective leader. Learn to watch your room and adjust your teaching style and techniques to fit the needs of your audience. (See item 35 of this book: *Vary Your Teaching Styles*.)

> *There is nothing concealed that will not be disclosed, or hidden that will not be made known. What I tell you in the dark, speak in the daylight; what is whispered in your ear....* Matthew 10:26–27

Adjust your teaching style and techniques to fit the needs of your audience.

79. Using the Bible in your group meetings – Have your Bible open, refer to the Bible, quote from the Bible, or have a group member read a Bible verse out loud in group. This shows the group clearly that these are not your own words; rather they are God's Spirit-filled words directly from the Bible. Learn to drive home a key point from your study using the Bible. It is our guidebook to life. Encourage group members to have their quiet times at home, marinating in the Bible and memorizing verses, which become tools in their toolbox. Soon they will be quoting from the Bible and underlining impactful verses in their Bible. Know that your group members are watching *you* closely, hungry to learn and grow! Know that your group members will model what they see you do as good and trusted leader.

Know that your group members are watching *you* closely, hungry to learn and grow!

> *My son, keep my words and store up my commands within you. Keep my commands and you will live; guard my teachings as the apple of your eye. Bind them on your fingers; write them on the tablet of your heart.* Proverbs 7:1–3

80. Be a very good listener – Listening is a skill. Studies show most of us are not listening clearly. To quote the book, *The Sacred Art of Listening* by Kay Lindahl, "...we are distracted, preoccupied, or forgetful about 75 percent of the time. Marketing studies indicate that the average attention span for adults is 22 seconds." Often we are distracted by the busyness of life. Usually we are totally absorbed in our own thoughts, thinking about how we would respond to what is being said. Many times you may simply not be paying attention to those in speaking in front of you. Perhaps you are bored of them, or feel you already know what they will say next. An example might be when we multi-task; working on the computer, watching a sports game, and trying to listen to someone at the same time. You can't do so many things at once, and what usually happens is that your listening skills suffer.

The good news is that we can learn or re-learn the valuable skill of listening. Discipline your mind to focus on what is being said, trying not to get distracted. A suggestion to help with improving your listening skill is to use *the 3 R's of listening*: repeat, rephrase, and reflect on what the person in front of you is saying. It may be important to unlearn some poor habits and create better listening habits. Another *key* is to be a double-question asker. For example, you might ask the person in front of you: "How are you doing?" A common answer given is "I'm doing fine," or "I'm doing great!" These are superficial answers, and oftentimes they may be untrue and unrealistic. Learn to *be a double-question asker.* Ask a second question such as; "So, can you tell me about how you are really doing?" Let the person in front of you know you care! Share with them that you truly care and are wondering how they're dealing with such and such a problem. It will take an extra few moments, but good listening helps build relationships, and relationships are a key part to leadership. Try these suggestions and with focus you can improve your leadership skills.

> *My son, if you accept my words and store up my commands*
> *within you, turning your ear to wisdom, and applying*
> *your heart to understanding...* Proverbs 2:1–2

81. Know Jesus Christ is a practical leader – Our greatest teacher on Earth, Jesus Christ, was a very practical leader. He taught life lessons when, where, and about life as he walked this Earth. Learn to make your study an everyday practical message, which group members can identify with, grasp, and relate to their own life. I encourage you to make your messages practical, simple, and realistic. Make them "mash potatoes and gravy" style teachings, which are practical and insightful.

Come to me, all you who are weary and burdened, and I will give you rest. Take my yoke upon you and learn from me, for I am gentle and humble in heart, and you will find rest for your souls. For my yoke is easy and my burden is light. Matthew 11:28

82. Be okay with not knowing everything – It's okay to say to a member of the group, "I don't know the answer; Can I get back to you this week?" Alternatively you can say "Let's continue this conversation after the group meeting." if you don't have the time to get into a lengthy conversation about something that may not pertain to the group. If you say you are going to get back to a group member, it is important to follow through and contact them during the next week.

I will strengthen them in the Lord and in his name they will walk... Zechariah 10:12

If the ax is dull and its edge unsharpened, more strength is needed but skill will bring success. Ecclesiastes 10:10

Teamwork

83. Focus on God in the group – The focus in your small group or support group should be on God first. Questions to ask include: "What does God want you to do?" and "What does God want you to learn?" If a group member is dealing with a situation; what is the group member's part that God may want him or her take responsibility for?

By wisdom a house is built, and through understanding it is established; through knowledge its rooms are filled with rare and beautiful treasures. Proverbs 24:3–4

84. Encourage the members of your group – You could be the only godly person that a group member knows, or the only loving friend that a group member is getting help from in this season of life. Love those in your group and encourage them to be all they can be for the glory of God.

As iron sharpens iron, so on man sharpens another. Proverbs 27:17

85. Begin and end meetings in prayer – The most powerful tool you have is prayer! Open and end your group meeting in prayer. Know the power of the Holy Spirit is the key which opens the hearts of group members. Rotating the opening and closing prayers for your meetings, is a simple way that group members can feel a part of the group and take ownership for encouraging the group. Also, this is an effective way for a group member to start feeling more comfortable about praying openly. Initially, some may be uncomfortable, but they will adjust. They are attending the group meeting to learn and to see, hear, and share what is on their heart. Your job is to help open the "doors of their heart" with the help of the Holy Spirit. As your group meeting ends, close in prayer showing reverence, respect, and humility to God. This closing prayer is a simple way to let God work in and through the group members in the next week, with the help of the Holy Spirit.

> **Your job is to help open the "doors of their heart" with the help of the Holy Spirit.**

Then you will call upon me and find me when you seek me with all your heart. I will be found by you, declares the Lord... Jeremiah 29:13

...of the Holy Spirit, and teaching them to everything I have commanded you. And surely I am with you always, to the very end of the age. Matthew 28:19–20

86. Focus on relationships in your group – A large portion of people in today's fast-paced society are simply not expressing their real feelings and emotions. Oftentimes we can be caught up in the busyness of life and frustrated with different areas of life. We may feel a basic need to be heard. Your group meeting can be a valuable setting where group members can develop the habit of being real and communicating better in a safe place with others. It is important that you create an atmosphere in your group(s) in which your group members can learn to communicate openly and relate better with those in the group. The members of the group can learn, or re-learn and practice group and individual communication skills. As a result, group members will have better relationships with their spouses and children, or others they interact with throughout their day. Model to your group the important skill of relating to others, slowing down the pace of life, and relating to others as God intended us to.

> *Two are better than one, because they have a good return for their work; if one falls down, his friend can help him up. But pity the man who falls and has no one to help him up!* Ecclesiastes 4:9–10

87. Maintain consistency in regular weekly meetings – In the midst of a crisis, an hour, a day, or a week can be a very long time. A group member might be in the middle of a divorce, separated from their spouse or kids, losing their job, have a very serious illness, be uprooted from their home, or any number of life's challenges. It is important to have a consistent regular meeting day and time that group members can look forward to.

> *Trust in the Lord with all your heart and lean not on your own understanding; in all ways acknowledge him, and he will make your paths straight.* Proverbs 3:5–6

88. Promote a safe group environment – The group needs to be a safe place for group members to share. Stress that, unless it is a life-threatening situation, what is discussed in the group stays in the group! It is important that confidentially be imbedded into your group. A simple confidentially form can help with this and enforce this key group principle. A confidentiality form should be signed and dated by each group member. **See a sample copy at the back of this workbook.**

It is important that confidentially be imbedded into your group.

> *What you heard from me, keep as the pattern of sound teaching, with faith and love in Christ Jesus. Guard the good deposit that was entrusted to you—guard it with the help of the Holy Spirit who lives in us.* 2 Timothy 1:13–14

89. Have a passion for your ministry and your group – It is important to have a passion for your God-given ministry and group. If you are not 100 percent sold out to your church, your ministry, and your group, you will need to think twice about being involved in it. Ministry can be very demanding, but extremely rewarding for those passionate about their God-given ministry and purpose.

However, I consider my life worth nothing to me, if only I may finish the race and complete the task the Lord Jesus has given me—the task of testifying to the gospel of God's grace. Acts 20:24

It is important to have a passion for your God-given ministry

90. Pray for wisdom and discernment – Most of us are all just ordinary people, who are asked to do extraordinary things, with eternal consequences. Pray over and over for God's wisdom and discernment, and he will make you wiser and more discerning in your ministry.

God's wisdom is profound, his power is vast. Who has resisted him and come out unscathed? Job 9:4

Therefore everyone who hears these words of mine and puts them into practice is like a wise man who built his house on the rock. Matthew 7:24

91. Welcome new members with open arms – Most new members will have all they can to deal with walking through the meeting room doors of a new group. They may be feeling lost, alone, in shock, embarrassed, or experiencing any number of feelings. Make new members feel welcome. With a smile on your face, provide them with your study, introductory information, phone list, etc. Let them know on their first visit, that they are important to you and that you care about their problems.

For he will be like a refiner's fire or launderer's soap. He will sit as a refiner and purifier of silver; he will purify... and refine them like gold and silver. Malachi 3:2–3

92. Read group guidelines periodically – As you have new members joining the group, it is important to review the list of group guidelines during group meetings, so new members know how the group operates and what is expected of them. **See a sample list of guidelines in the back of this workbook.** Emphasize that there will be no cross talk and no disruptive interruptions during group meetings. Members should try to be respectful of the leadership team, even if they do not always agree with a leader's point of view.

To do what is right and just is more acceptable to
the Lord than sacrifice. Proverbs 21:3

93. Have a group phone list and encourage group connection – It is very important to pass out a confidential group roster to encourage the members of the group to meet with each other or to call each other during the week. A phone roster and email list is easy to create and can be passed out periodically. It should not be considered as a contact list to promote any type of business dealings. Group members meeting for coffee, having lunch or dinner, attending church services together, or going to the movies together creates a sense of community in the group. Delegate someone to take charge of group activities. This may be something as simple as a phone call to a couple of the group members during the week to help group members feel connected.

Let us not give up meeting together, as some are in the
habit of doing, but let us encourage one another—and all the more as
you see the Day approaching. Hebrews 10:25

94. Take group attendance – It is important to take group attendance weekly, updating contact information accurately. This it helps each group member feel a part of the group. If a new member is not on the updated group list, he might feel like an outsider and not part of their new-found group. This is something very simple, which might take away an excuse why a new member may not come back. Go out of your way to make new members feel welcome. Another good reason to take attendance is that your church also could ask you to turn in weekly or monthly attendance records, for budget reasons, room scheduling reasons, etc.

If we walk in the light, as God is in the light,
we have fellowship with one another. 1 John 1:7

95. Ideal sharing size is 4 to 8 members – During your group meetings, dividing into small table discussion groups will allow for more personal discussion of the study or what is going on in the lives of group members. Three or four is not too small for a table discussion group. In fact, your table discussion groups will have more time to go deeper into the concerns that group member's had during the previous week. With eight or more in one table discussion group, it would be best to split the group into smaller table discussion groups, (this is done after you have a twenty to thirty minute study for the larger overall group). This splitting up into multiple table discussion groups gives group members more opportunity to share and potential co-leaders a chance to grow and learn as they lead the smaller table discussion groups. Don't try to control everything and be everywhere at once. Let go of your support group, letting others take ownership through their table discussion groups. As group members connect and learn during their table discussions, the overall larger group will grow, impacting more lives for eternity more than you can imagine.

> Don't try to control everything and be everywhere at once.

A man of many companions may come to ruin, but there is a friend who sticks closer than a brother. Proverbs 18:24

III. CONCLUSION

Some of these leadership tools will serve you best if you marinate your mind on them from time to time. As you step into a leadership role, you will grow, mature, and increase in confidence. Your role may change in the weeks and months to follow. Know that God will help you mature spiritually with the power of the Holy Spirit. With these valuable leadership tools under your belt, your role and skills as a confident leader will come alive, as your group experience builds, defining who and where you are in ministry.

I encourage you to share these valuable tools with other leaders, so they may also share in God's wisdom and discerning Spirit.

Commit to the Lord whatever you do, and your plans will succeed.
Proverbs 16:3

THERE ARE NO LIMITS

There are no limits
with God.
His resources are far beyond
your abilities.
Never say, "I can't"
without saying, "he can."
Never feel you are weak
without knowing that he is strong.
You will never have to hold back
or turn back
because of fear,
for he is with you...
you will never have to be defeated,
because his victory is yours...
you will never have to settle
for the ordinary,
because his life is extraordinary.

By Roy Lessin

Not only was the Teacher wise, but also he imparted knowledge to the people. He pondered and searched out and set in order many proverbs. The Teacher searched to find just the right words and what he wrote was upright and true. The words of the wise are like goads, their collected sayings like firmly embedded nails-given by one Shepherd. Be warned, my son, of anything in addition to them.
Ecclesiastes 12:9–12

APPENDIX

Wisdom Keys of Jesus

During your personal journey into leadership, learn to marinate on God's Word and different inspirational books. An example of this is the motivational book, *The Leadership Secrets of Jesus*, by Mike Murdock (Honor Books, 1997). Here are a few truths, along with supporting Scripture from the book, which can help shape your leadership skills.

- **You will never change your life until you change something you do daily.** I've discovered that developing healthy spiritual habits verifies God's transformation in our lives.

- **You will always remember what you teach.** We don't always remember what we're taught, but in order to teach others we must work the message into our minds and hearts. *Instruct a wise man, and he will be wiser still; teach a righteous man, and he will add to his learning.* Proverbs 9:9

- **Jesus knew that every great achievement requires a willingness to begin small.** *The wisdom of the prudent is to give thought to their ways.* Proverbs 14:8

- **When you decide what you want, the "how to do it" will emerge.** Every plan starts with a desire to accomplish something.

- **Your rewards in life are determined by the problems you solve for someone else.** Serving others is greater than any material accomplishment.

- **Silence cannot be misquoted—no words needed.**

- **The problem that infuriates you the most is the problem God has assigned you to solve.** What we do today paves the way for someone else tomorrow. *Do not be deceived; God is not mocked. A man reaps what he sows.* Galatians 6:7

- **When you want something you have never had, you have got to do something you have never done.** A life well lived always involves risks.

- **Your success depends on timing.** And God is in charge of timing.

- **Your future is determined by the seeds you sow today.** Don't be afraid to plant or you'll never have a garden.

- **When God talks, the wise listen. Be wise.** *Your word is a lamp to my feet, and a light for my path.* Psalm 119:105

- **Your greatest mistakes will happen because of impatience.** Learn the wisdom of prayer and timing in the decisions you make.

- **You will begin to succeed with your life when the hurt and problems of others begin to matter to you.** Selfishness gains us nothing in the end. *There is a time for everything; and a season for every activity under heaven.* Ecclesiastes 3:1

- **All men fall. The great ones get back up.** Where are you right now? *Stay away from a foolish man, for you will not find knowledge on his lips.* Proverbs 14:7

- **Great men simply have great habits.** What do your habits say about you?

- **Planning is the starting point for any dream or goal that you possess.** What's on your drawing board?

- **Successes are usually scheduled events.** Failures are not. Learn from life's unexpected moments. *He has made everything beautiful in its time.* Ecclesiastes 3:11

- **You will never possess what you are unwilling to pursue.** What is it worth to you to have it?

- **Your integrity will always be remembered longer than your product.** Are you a man who is trusted by others?

- **Jesus was honest.** Does your life reflect Christ to others? *Do not repay anyone evil for evil. Be careful to do what is right.* Romans 12:17

- **Sometimes you have to do things you hate to create something you love.** True joy rarely comes without some kind of pain.

- The quality of preparation determines the quality of performance. *Whatever you do, work at it with all your heart, as working for the Lord, not for men.* Colossians 3:23

- **You will only have significant success with something that is an obsession.** Mild interest is not enough.

- **You will always move toward anyone who increases you and away from anyone who decreases you.** Are there areas in your life where you feel attraction or resistance? Pay attention.

- **Stop looking at where you have been and start looking at where you are going.** God doesn't care where you've been; he only cares where you're headed.

- **Mentorship is the master key to extraordinary success.**

Learn to share the valuable God-given discerning wisdom, with those you touch in life.

As we close this section, know you will not get very far in ministry without: 1) resting on God's power, 2) his incredible resourcefulness in your ministry, 3) your family, and 4) facing life's challenges in the mist of ministry. Learn that God can open doors so easily. God can use a leader's weakness to accomplish his purpose.

You will not get very far in ministry without resting on God's power.

He said to me, "My grace is sufficient for you, for my power is made perfect in weakness." Therefore I will boast all the more gladly about my weaknesses, so that Christ's power may rest on me. That is why, for Christ's sake, I delight in weaknesses, in insults, in hardships, in persecutions, in difficulties. For when I am weak, then I am strong.
2 Corinthians 12:9–10

Your Lifetime Purpose and Goals

When in leadership, or considering stepping into group leadership, your lifetime purpose and goals are very important. They help you to see who you are, and where you fit in your God-given ministry. Pray day after day, challenging God, to show you his purpose for your life and ministry. Pray, meditate, and write down what you feel God's plan is for your life on Earth. (Please pull out additional paper as you write your purpose and goals.)

What is your God-given purpose or purposes here on Earth?

_____

_____

_____

_____

_____

_____

List your God-inspired ministry goals for the next year.

_____

_____

_____

_____

_____

_____

List your God-inspired ministry goals for the next five years.

_____

_____

_____

_____

_____

Keys for Good Listening

1. **Be Quiet and Listen**

   Allow group members to share, maybe 10 to 15 minutes each.

2. **Give the Person Speaking Freedom to Share**

   Help group members feel comfortable about sharing their true feelings.

3. **Be an Engaged Listener**

   Strive to understand the group member. Look at them while they talk and express interest.

4. **Help Minimize Distractions**

   Shut off cell phones, laptops, minimize noise in the meeting room, and avoid any unnecessary shuffling of papers.

5. **Be Empathetic as You Listen**

   Learn to care about the person in front of you!

6. **Be an Understanding Listener, Trying not to Interrupt**

   Allow the group member to share without interruption. Be patient and ask questions with interest and consider your timing.

7. **Don't Get Angry About What is Said**

   Do not let a group member get the best of you; be slow to anger, quick to listen.

Keys for Good Listening (continued)

8. **Try Not to be Critical or Appear Judgmental.**

   Try not to be confrontational or argumentative with group members, as group meetings are not the proper format for confrontation.

9. **Ask Good Questions**

   Encourage sharing that will help lead group members to answer their own questions and promote thought-provoking dialog and sharing. You cannot solve a group member's problems. Learn that a secret to leadership is to ask good questions.

10. **Let Others Share From Their Hearts**

    Again, stop talking so others can share from their hearts. As you learn the skill of listening from the heart, you will pass this valuable skill on to others through your example.

Small Group Guidelines

1. Group meetings should be set weekly, at a scheduled time.

2. Confidentiality is a requirement of any group conversation.

3. Sharing time limit is approximately 10 to15 minutes per person, based on available time.

4. No side conversations while someone is sharing.

5. Avoid interrupting others when someone is sharing.

6. No advice-giving to others.

7. Share in the first person ("It has been my experience that…").

8. Be a good listener.

9. Speak from the heart.

10. No poor or coarse language is to be used.

11. Arrive on time. Late arrivals to group meetings should try not to be disruptive.

12. Group members should respect the guidelines and guidance of their small group leader, even if they don't agree.

Confidentiality Policy

For Church Use Only

NAME (Please Print): _____

ADDRESS: _____

CITY, ZIP CODE: _____

TELEPHONE NUMBERS: _____

E-MAIL ADDRESS: _____

As a participant in this small group, I understand that this needs to be a safe place for myself and others to share. I agree to keep all conversations that occur within my small group in strict confidence.

I understand that I will be encouraged to focus on my growth and recovery in this season of my life.

I am willing to be contacted by the small group leadership team on an occasional basis for support. _____Yes _____No

I am willing to have my name and telephone number released to my small group leaders for encouragement and support. _____Yes _____No

Signed: _____ Date: _____

Notes: _____

_____

_____

_____

_____

_____

Sign In Sheet

(Information to be kept confidential)

Group Name: _____   Date: _____

Name	Address	Phone/Cell #	Email

Small Group Prayer Requests

(Information to be kept confidential)

Group Name: _____ Date: _____

Name	Prayer Request

Suggested Reading List

1. The Purpose Driven Life Rick Warren

2. The Master Plan of Evangelism Robert E. Coleman

3. The Leadership Secrets of Jesus Mike Murdock

4. My Utmost for His Highest Oswald Chambers

5. The Jesus I Never Knew Phillip Yancey

6. The Power of Integrity John F. Mac Arthur

7. Half Time Bob Buford

8. God's Words of Life for Leaders Zondervan

9. Lord Change Me! Evelyn Christenson

10. The Purpose Driven Church Rick Warren

11. The Prayer of Jabez Bruce H. Wilkerson

12. Teaching With Style (Tape Series) Bruce H. Wilkerson

Web Resources

1. BibleGateway.com   http://www.biblegateway.com

2. Celebrate Recovery   http://www.celebraterecovery.com

3. Smalley Marriage Institute http://www.smalleymarriage.com

4. Our Daily Bread   http://www.rbc.org/odb

5. Focus on the Family   http://www.family.org

6. Love and Respect   http://www.loveandrespect.com

7. Marriage Builders   http://www.marriagebuilders.com

8. Pastors.com   http://www.pastors.com

9. Purpose Driven Home   http://www.purposedriven.com

10. Purpose Driven Life   http://www.purposedrivenlife.com

11. Saddleback Church   http://www.saddleback.com

12. Walk in the Word   http://www.walkintheword.com

About the Author
Gary Hoffman

Gary Hoffman is a marital crisis survivor and leader of the Men on the Edge Ministry at Saddleback Church in Lake Forest, CA. Serving God by helping men develop God-centered relationships is a key purpose in my life. I started with little to no experience in leading others in small groups and now have more than 20 years experience in participating in and leading support groups, small groups, and men's groups of various kinds at Saddleback Church. I have learned, studied, and uncovered many success keys to small group leadership. Over time, I compiled a list of key leadership and mentoring guidelines that I have found successful in my own teaching and ministry.

God has provided me with a teaching team that currently teaches, mentors, and encourages men on a weekly basis, sharing with hundreds of men annually in the "Men On The Edge" programs taught at Saddleback Church and other locations. Every week we see God's hand at work helping men grow in their relationships.

If you would like to start a Men on the Edge group of your own, or desire someone to speak at your church or ministry venue, please contact:

Gary Hoffman, ghoffman@menontheedge.com
Jim Zoval, jzoval@menontheedge.com

Both can also be reached at:
949-709-7401
PO Box 283
Trabuco Canyon, CA 92678
www.MenOnTheEdge.com

INDEX

MEN ON THE EDGE
QUICK ORDER FORM

To order online go to www.MenOnTheEdge.com

Please send the following books and workbooks:

Title	Qty	Price
Don't Give Up Book, $12.98	_____	_____
Don't Give Up Workbook, $9.98	_____	_____
Leader Guide: Leadership Secrets to Success, $11.98	_____	_____

Sub-total _____

Add 7.75% for shipments to California _____

Shipping: Any 2 books $5.00, _____
   3 or more books, contact us (see below)

Order Total _____

PLEASE PRINT

Name: _____

Address: _____

City: _____ State: _____ Zipcode: _____

Phone: _____

E-mail: _____

Mail Orders with payment to:

> Men on the Edge
> PO Box 283
> Trabuco Canyon, CA 92678

Please send me FREE information on:

❏ Other Books   ❏ Speaking/Seminars
❏ Consulting   ❏ A Group Near Me
❏ Starting a Group

For volume shipping and book order quotes,
e-mail ghoffman@menontheedge.com.

Fax requests for information to: 949-951-0667

To order online go to www.MenOnTheEdge.com

MEN ON THE EDGE
QUICK ORDER FORM

To order online go to www.MenOnTheEdge.com

Please send the following books and workbooks:

Title	Qty	Price
Don't Give Up Book, $12.98	_____	_____
Don't Give Up Workbook, $9.98	_____	_____
Leader Guide: Leadership Secrets to Success, $11.98	_____	_____

Sub-total _____

Add 7.75% for shipments to California _____

Shipping: Any 2 books $5.00, _____

    3 or more books, contact us (see below)

                                Order Total _____

PLEASE PRINT

Name: _____

Address: _____

City: _____ State: _____ Zipcode: _____

Phone: _____

E-mail: _____

Mail Orders with payment to:

    Men on the Edge
    PO Box 283
    Trabuco Canyon, CA 92678

Please send me FREE information on:

❑ Other Books   ❑ Speaking/Seminars
❑ Consulting   ❑ A Group Near Me
❑ Starting a Group

For volume shipping and book order quotes,
e-mail ghoffman@menontheedge.com.

Fax requests for information to: 949-951-0667

To order online go to www.MenOnTheEdge.com

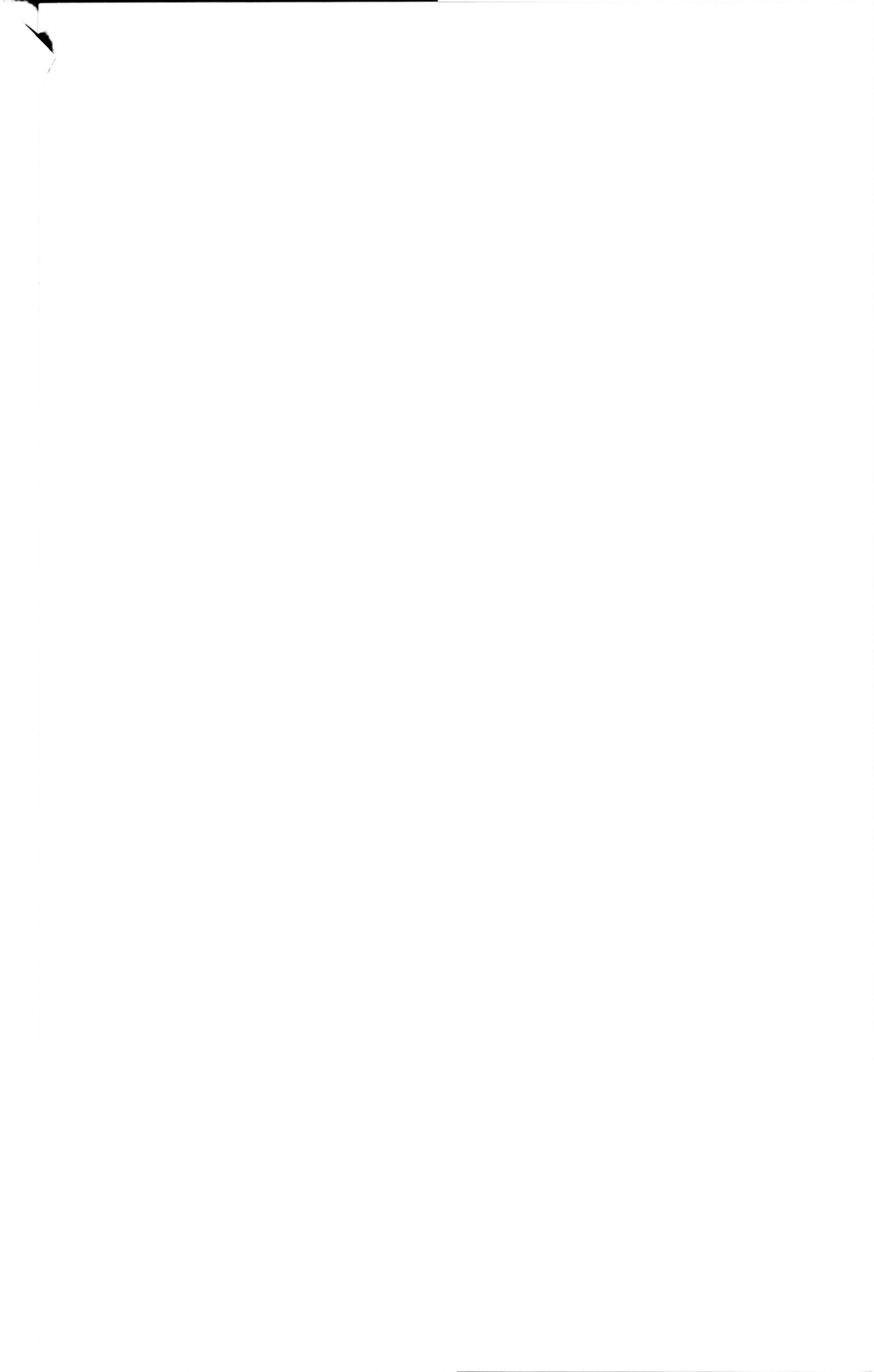

www.ingramcontent.com/pod-product-compliance
Lightning Source LLC
Chambersburg PA
CBHW062026040426
42447CB00010B/2161